Positive Affirmations for Little Boys

The ABC Book of Rhymes

SARAH MAZOR

Illustrator: Kathleen S. Mallari

AUTHOR'S NOTE

Positive affirmations work! I know because I and my children experience their magic first hand. Positive self-affirmations promote self-esteem, self-confidence, and an improved self-image. But the magic does not end there. Enhanced self-regard is even further rewarded as family, friends and acquaintances respond in kind. There is much truth in the old adage that claims: "Laugh and the world laughs with you."

Self-doubt does not begin in adulthood. Self-esteem challenges and conversely a positive self-image can often be attributed to early childhood experiences. Thus, promoting self-confidence and self-appreciation and a positive attitude toward the self during the early years of life is of supreme importance.

Read *Positive Affirmations for Little Boys: The ABC Book of Rhymes* with your son, grandson, nephew or favorite godchild. The beloved little boy in your life deserves a bright future and you can help her achieve just that.

Acquire the *Positive Affirmations for Little Girls: The ABC Book of Rhymes* and contribute to the emotional health of a beloved little girl. The girls' edition is available on Amazon.com

With gratitude,
Sarah Mazor

Thank you for buying

Positive Affirmations
for Little Boys

I hope you enjoy the book and
and read it often!

Check out the Girls' Edition
on Amazon.com

Aa

Adorable

I make faces, I giggle
I jump high and I wiggle
I am happy, you see
I am, ADORABLE me

Bb

Brotherly

I love my baby brother, he's so small
I hold his hand so he won't fall
I am happy, you see
I am, BROTHERLY me

Curious

I ask, I inquire
To learn is my desire
I am happy, you see
I am, CURIOUS me

Darling

I am loved, I love back
I so love my uncle Jack
I am happy, you see
I am, DARLING me

Ee

Excellent

I tidy my desk, I tidy my bed
I put things away like Mommy said
I am happy, you see
I am, EXCELLENT me

Ff

Fearless

I am strong, I am brave
Fun adventures I crave
I am happy, you see
I am, FEARLESS me

Generous

I share my lunch with little Trudi
I even share my chocolate goodie
I am happy, you see
I am, GENEROUS me

Hh

Healthy

I jump rope, I run, I play
I exercise every day
I am happy, you see
I am, HEALTHY me

Ii

Imaginative

I tell magic stories and funny tales
Of mermaids, dolphins and whales
I am happy, you see
I am, IMAGINATIVE me

Joyous

When I play with Lil the cat
On the playroom's little mat
I am happy, you see
I am, JOYOUS me

Kindhearted

I gave my toy to Lilly May
Who broke her foot the other day
I am happy, you see
I am, KINDHEARTED me

Ll

Lovable

Mommy hugs me, oh so tight
Daddy calls me his delight
I am happy, you see
I am, LOVABLE me

Mm

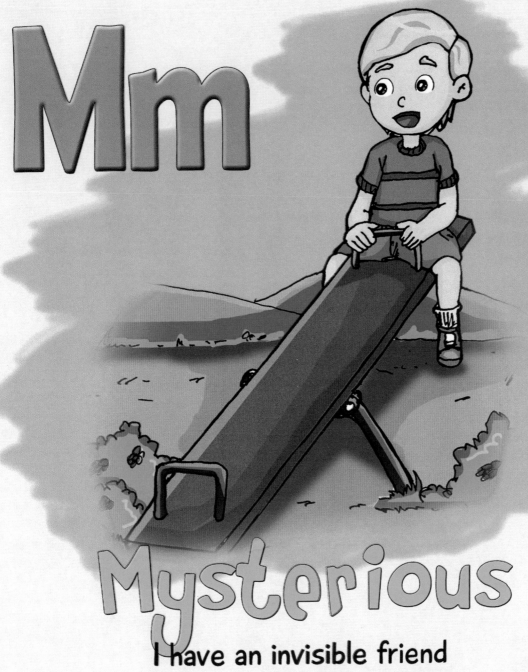

Mysterious

I have an invisible friend
With whom I play pretend
I am happy, you see
I am, MYSTERIOUS me

Nn

WELCOME

Neighborly

I visit friends next door
I play with Eric, he is four
I am happy, you see
I am, NEIGHBORLY me

Oo

Optimistic

I am joyful, life is good
I'm always in a cheery mood
I am happy, you see
I am, OPTIMISTIC me

Pp

Polite

I say thank you, I say please
And God bless you when you sneeze
I am happy, you see
I am, POLITE me

Quick

I run, I race around the block
I am faster than Jacob and Brock
I am happy, you see
I am, Quick me

Rr

Remarkable

I sing, I draw, I dance, I write
Always an artist, day and night
I am happy, you see
I am, REMARKABLE me

Ss

Silly

I like acting a little zany
Even though I am quite brainy
I am happy, you see
I am, SILLY me

Tt

Truthful

What did I do today and why?
I'll tell you all, I do not lie
I am happy, you see
I am, TRUTHFUL me

Uu

Unique

My sister, my brother and I make three
But I am the one and only me
I am happy, you see
I am, UNIQUE me

Vv

Valuable

I am a blessing, says my mother
Like my sister and my brother
I am happy, you see
I am, VALUABLE me

Wonderful

I am lovable, sweet and kind
The best that you may find
I am happy, you see
I am, WONDERFUL me

(e)Xtraordinary

I asked the letter X to ask the letter E
To let it use an E word, to tell about me
I am happy, you see
I am, (e)XTRAORDINARY me

Yummy

I ate some ice cream with sugar and spice
It spilled on me, I smell so nice
I am happy, you see
I am, YUMMY me

I learned a new word, oh my
It begins with a Z and ends with a Y
I am happy, you see
I am, ZIPPY (full of energy) me

And Start All Over Again!

ABOUT THE AUTHOR

Sarah Mazor is a mother, an entrepreneur and a personal coach who holds an undergraduate degree in business journalism and master's degree in psychology. The MazorBooks publishing effort affords Sarah the opportunity to combine her many interests in a project that encompasses her love for children and her love for books. The books Sarah publishes through MazorBooks aim to provide children and parents hours bonding time as well as a fun ways to promote children's cognitive abilities and enhance their self-confidence and self-esteem.

The MazorBooks Library
Children's Books with Good Values

www.MazorBooks.com
http://mazorbooks.wordpress.com

Smart Kids Bright Future Children's Books Collection
- ABC Book of Rhymes *by Mark Eichler*
- The Hebrew Alphabet: Book of Rhymes for English Speaking Kids, *by Yael Rosenberg and Sarah Mazor*
- Little Rose Learns to Count *by Mark Eichler*
- Little Shani Learns to Count (Hebrew Edition) *by Mark Eichler*
- Modes of Transportation : ABC Book of Rhymes *by Sarah Mazor and Yael Rosenbreg*
- Positive Affirmations for Little Boys: The ABC Book of Rhymes *by Sarah Mazor*
- Positive Affirmations for Little Girls: The ABC Book of Rhymes *by Sarah Mazor*
- What I Want to Be When I Grow Up *by Michali Mazor*

Smart Kids Healthy Kids Children's Books Collection
- Nurse Olivia "Liv" Welle Presents: Who Knew Vitamins Could Be Fun *by Yael Rosenberg*

Smart Kids Bedtime Stories Children's Books Collection
- A Bully in Monkeyville *by Ari Mazor*
- Brian Learns to Tell Time *by Mark Eichler*
- Clothes Have Feelings Too! Charlie Learns to Care for His Things *by Ari Mazor*
- I Want to Pet the Ducks: Abey Goes to Washington *by Mark Eichler*
- I Want to Pet the Fish: Abey Visits the Aquarium *by Mark Eichler*
- Little Rose's Big Lie. *by Shani Eichler (Coming Soon)*
- Oh No! There Are Monsters in My Room *by Mark Eichler*

Made in the USA
Lexington, KY
07 February 2017